BREAKING THE ALABASTAR BOX

ISBN 978-0-557-27930-2

BREAKING THE ALABASTER BOX

Intimacy With Jesus Through Prayer
Lesson 1: Prayer is Fellowship; Prayer is Worship

Matthew 26:6 Now when Jesus was in Bethany, in
the house of Simon the leper,
7 There came unto him a woman having an
alabaster box of very precious ointment, and poured
it on his head, as he sat at meat.

Mary's spontaneous act of love and worship is memorialized through the ages. We are all familiar with this beautiful story. How perfect her worship was; how pure her love for Jesus! Mary's act of devotion is also the perfect expression of prayer.

How would you define prayer? Some people see prayer as a necessary religious ritual. For others, prayer is a laundry list of requests. Many of us experience prayer as a boring and tedious obligation. As Mary so eloquently expressed, prayer is much more than these. Prayer is intimate fellowship with our Savior. Prayer is worship.* Prayer is a love song to Jesus.

In order to experience the beauty and power of effective prayer, we must change the way we view prayer. Have you ever been in love? Do you remember the eager anticipation of every moment you spent with your Beloved? The agony you felt when you were apart. He was on your mind every moment of your day and filled your dreams at night. And when you were with him, the joy almost hurt as it filled your whole being.*

That is what Mary felt as she poured the spikenard over her Beloved's feet. Those tears were tears of joy. Mary did not care who saw or who criticized. She was in the presence of the One who filled her heart. That is the experience of prayer. Prayer is pure worship.

When we worship publicly, we are part of a corporate celebration. It is somewhat like a family reunion. When my great-grandmother was alive, every family reunion centered around her as the matriarch of our clan. Jesus is the center of our assemblies. Corporate worship is joyful indeed. But nothing can take the place of the sweet, tender intimacy of the prayer closet. There, we are alone with the Beloved, holding hands, whispering confidences. How wonderful that the God of the Church is also the God of the saint. Jesus did not just die for his Bride, he died for me. In prayer, we conduct our personal relationship with the most important person in our lives.*

Sometimes we tend to think of personal prayer as secondary to attending church or giving time and money to God. Sadly, we sometimes think of it as an optional addition to our Christian lives; meant for those who are spiritually superior. Nothing could be farther from the truth. Not only is prayer available to every Christian; it is essential to salvation. It is the foundation of being a Child of God; we will not make heaven without it.*

Can you imagine being married and never spending time alone with your husband? How long do you suppose that marriage would last? What if the only time your husband ever said, "I love you" was when he wanted something? If communication is essential to a marriage, it is essential to maintaining a relationship with our Lord. In fact, prayer is much more essential than we often understand.

Prayer is the underpinning for everything spiritual in our lives. Without prayer, our church attendance is merely participation in a social club. Without prayer, we will never understand our purpose for being on earth at all. When you see a Christian who is always offended, and never feels others in the church are treating them right, you see a person with no prayer life. And that person whose anointed ministry you admire - she found it in the place of prayer.*

It cannot be emphasized too strongly. EVERYTHING spiritual begins in prayer. Do you need a financial blessing? You cannot wait to develop a personal relationship with Jesus until you need something. That relationship must be already developed before the need arises. Do you want to be used of God? God chooses those for service whose heart is in tune with his. This happens in prayer.

If you want to feel the Spirit in the worship service, you must learn to feel it on your knees. If you want to have peace in the storm, you must pray through the storm. All the blessings of salvation come from spending time with the Savior.

Prayer is not only important, prayer is a privilege. It is a joy. Have you ever imagined what you will do when you meet Jesus face to face? Have you longed to spend time with him and ask him deep questions? Well, you can. God has designed prayer to be a loving, intimate place where you can be alone with him. In the place of prayer, each of us takes priority in God's agenda; we have his ear. God delights in our time with him and he always listens. He never gets impatient at hearing the same needs over and over. He is never too busy to stop and listen. He is saddened when we neglect him.*

God longs to share his intimate secrets with us, but he cannot share with us if we do not share with him. What beautiful revelations we might have received if we had given him first place in our time!

Jesus is waiting to hear from you. He longs to bless you and teach you. He wants to hear every problem and every dream. Your Savior wants to be your best friend. Don't keep him waiting!

Discussion

1. `Are you satisfied with your personal prayer life? Why or why not?
2. What would you like to change about your prayer life?
3. How would you describe your relationship with Jesus?

Exercises

1. Think of those things you have never shared with anyone. Write them down. Every hidden secret, every private dream. Title it "Things to Discuss With Jesus."

2. Make another list. This one is a list of every question for which you would like an answer.

3. On another paper, write down everything Jesus has done for you. Draw a line down the middle and make a list of all the things you would like to do for Him.

4. Find a private place. (the car, the bathroom, anywhere you can lock the door). Imagine that Jesus is sitting beside you. Share the lists with him. There is no right or wrong way to do it as long as you do it. He is anxious to hear from you.

Notes

BREAKING THE ALABASTER BOX

Lesson 2: Teach Us To Pray - Our Father

Matthew 6:9 After this manner therefore pray ye: Our
Father which art in heaven, Hallowed be thy name.
10 Thy kingdom come, Thy will be done in earth, as
it is in heaven.
11 Give us this day our daily bread.
12 And forgive us our debts, as we forgive our
debtors.
13 And lead us not into temptation, but deliver us
from evil: For thine is the kingdom, and the power,
and the glory, for ever. Amen.

The disciples had many opportunities to observe Jesus's prayer life. What they saw led them to the conclusion that the activity they had called prayer really wasn't prayer at all. They beseeched Jesus to teach them to pray. Jesus responded to the request by giving them the model prayer which we commonly refer to as "The Lord's Prayer".

It is important to remember that this is a model prayer. There is only limited benefit at best in just reciting the words themselves. Remember that prayer is an intimate conversation. It should be fresh each time and personal. The Lord's Prayer teaches us how to pray, not what to say.

Also, it is not always necessary to pray in the exact order of the model. Prayer should flow easily and the Spirit will guide you on your prayer journey. Jesus's model helps understand the components of prayer, to make us more comfortable in our conversations with God.

However we begin our prayer, we should speak to God as a child speaking to its father, for God is indeed "Our Father". This relationship is the basis for prayer and determines everything in our communication with God.

As our Father, God is eager to hear from us. He is responsible for meeting our needs and helping us grow. As a father, God must discipline us when we need it. Most of all, God wants to spend quality time with us.

Because we go to prayer as a child going to its father, we go boldly and in faith. Faith alone brings answers to our prayers and knowing that God is our parent builds our faith by assuring us of God's love.

Prayer is the acting out of our relationship with God. Our prayer time is just as much about telling God how much we love him as it is about getting our needs met. It should be natural for us to ask God's opinions and seek ways to please him. Spiritually, his children sit on his lap and talk intimately and freely.

How do we develop this intimacy in prayer which draws us closer to God?
First of all, we should drop all formality in prayer. Our prayers should be conversational. You see, spiritual growth is about increased relationship with God. Effective prayers are prayers filled with faith in our favor with God. Prayer should be like talking with a friend.

Since God is our father, he is also our provider. We can expect him to meet our needs because that is a father's job; indeed, a father's delight. We can be bold in presenting our requests. So when we pray, we should not hesitate to make not only our needs, but our desires known. However, we must always submit to our father's will. If we feel we must have a red Mustang convertible and God sends us a silver Hyundai, it is not that he does not love us. He is merely being a responsible parent who gives us what we need, not what we think we need. After all the bold requests, we should always say "Your will be done".

When we were small children, we thought our parents were invincible. We trusted that our parents were powerful enough to keep us safe. Some of us were disappointed in that trust. Some of us were betrayed by the very people we looked to for our safety and well being. Now we have a new parent, who is truly powerful and will never let us down. In prayer we place ourselves in the security of our Father's arms and we can have peace.

Discussion

1. What person in your life has been the most

instrumental in teaching you about prayer? How?

2. How has your relationship with God changed your definition of the word "father"?

3. What are some attributes of a good parent? How do these attributes relate to God?

4. What does God want from us?

5. Has God ever disappointed you? Has He ever let you down? Is there a difference?

Exercises

1. Close your eyes and remember a happy time from your childhood. Perhaps there was no happy time with your parents, but picture a time where an adult was good to you and where you had fun. Dwell on those happy feelings. Now picture yourself as a child in Heaven, having that good time with your Heavenly Father. Every time you pray, take that picture with you to build your faith and remind you of your relationship to God.

2. Make a list of the attributes of a good parent. Beside each attribute, write a time when God manifested that attribute in your life. Thank God for his role as your parent.

3. When you pray, picture yourself on your Father's lap. Tell him about your day. Ask for little blessings, not just necessities. Sing to him. Pretend that you are seven years old.

Notes

Breaking the Alabaster Box

Lesson 3: Teach Me to Pray - Who art in Heaven

Matthew 6:9 After this manner therefore pray ye: Our
Father which art in heaven, Hallowed be thy name.
10 Thy kingdom come, Thy will be done in earth, as
it is in heaven.
11 Give us this day our daily bread.
12 And forgive us our debts, as we forgive our
debtors.
13 And lead us not into temptation, but deliver us
from evil: For thine is the kingdom, and the power,
and the glory, for ever. Amen.

Our Father is a Heavenly Father. This means that God is not flesh and blood, but a Spirit. Although we are flesh and blood, we are created in his image. We have a spirit within us which can communicate with our father and feel his presence. It is our spirit, and not our intellect, that we use to fellowship with God in prayer.

Because God is spiritual, prayer must be spiritual. We must learn to listen to the Spirit within us using our spirit. To do this, we must learn to recognize the voice of the Spirit and how to respond with our spirit. This process is called faith, and faith is the method of converting fleshly emotions and needs into spiritual language.

You see, there is a barrier to our relationship with our Father. Although he is totally Spirit, we view the world through our bodily senses. Our human spirit has difficulty bypassing those senses. Paul said that communicating with and sensing God was like viewing a reflection in a mirror. We cannot see clearly. Oh, one day we will have a spiritual body and this barrier will be removed. Until that glorious day, we use faith..

Faith is the tool we use to cross the barriers between flesh and spirit. If we walked by sight, we would be certain of God's will every time we prayed. We could see him frown or smile and hear his words clearly in our ears. However, until we see our father face to face, we walk by faith and not by sight.

What is faith anyway? Is it just a mental belief? Faith is much more than that. Faith is a certainty based on a relationship. Faith comes, as the Bible tells us, by hearing the Word of God. In other words, God gives us a promise which we believe because of who God is. When we have a clear Word from God, we can have faith that will hold us through any storm until the answer comes.

Since faith is essential for prayer and faith comes by the Word, then the Word is essential for prayer. Each time we pray, we must bring to God's attention the promises he has already given us and stand boldly on those promises as we bring our needs to him. We must also seek a fresh Word. Thus we must pray with our Bible open.

This is one reason why we pray about the same thing more than once. As we pray, we are not simply repeating the same request over and over like a whiny child. Rather, we are seeking to understand the Lord's will in each of our needs. Each time we pray about something, we meditate on the Word and listen to the voice of the Holy Spirit. Each day we show our faith by acting on what the Word has shown us. When our will and His are identical, our faith looses the power of God into our lives.

Another reason faith is so essential for prayer is that we cannot see into the spiritual world. As soon as we pray, God responds. In Heaven, the answer is formed immediately. Our miracle is prepared and waiting. All it needs is for our faith to reach the proper level. But we cannot see what is taking place in Heaven. So as we wait, we believe nothing is happening. We need to release our faith to stand on the Word we have received and be convinced that though we cannot see what God is doing, it must be finished in Heaven and released by faith into the physical realm.

Repeatedly praying about the same need does not necessarily

indicate a lack of faith. Certainly, if our prayers are filled with doubt and anxiety, we do ourselves no good. But if each time we pray about something, we quote the word and declare our faith, then we lose God to work, first in Heaven, then on earth. We build our faith as we assert that our need is already met in the spiritual realm, even though we might not yet see it.

The spirit realm is God's realm. What he does there is perfect. When we pray, and our prayers reach Heaven, they are transformed into perfect prayers - ones that align with the perfect will of God. To perfect our faith, God will refine and teach us his will, in order that our will may align with his and be released first in the Spirit and then on the earth. We should expect God to change us before he answers us.

When we pray, we should not put God in a box by only giving him one way to answer us. Spiritual answers are perfect answers. God may surprise us by the direction from which our prayers are answered.

I have a dear friend who was experiencing mysterious health problems. She and I prayed together for miraculous healing. On her nest visit to the state's charity hospital where, since she, was uninsured she went for medical treatment, she had a long-awaited appointment with a dermatologist for what she thought were allergies. That dermatologist recognized the symptoms of thyroid disease and began to treat her personally. At a charity hospital, my sister was getting the treatment of a specialist for free! She was getting her thyroid medicine for free because she was part of a study and did not have to wait the long hours necessary to get in the regular clinics. Immediately her health improved.

But my friend did not want free medicine. She wanted the attention that came with a supernatural event. So after a young evangelist came through town claiming that no one with faith need ever be ill, my friend through away her medicine, claiming instant healing. And, you guessed it, her symptoms returned. You see, God had answered her prayer; just not the way she preferred. We have to trust that spiritual methods beat ours every time.

In summary, prayer is a spiritual activity, loosed first in

Heaven. Because we are earthen vessels, we must use faith to bridge the gap between Heaven and earth. We want to bring Heaven down and transform the earthly into the spiritual. Spiritual prayer is effectual prayer.

Discussion

1. What are some aspects of our human nature which hinder our hearing from God?

2. How does the Word of God give us faith?

3. How does continually praying for a need produce faith?

4. How do we learn God's will in a specific situation?

5. What are some ways that people limit God?

Exercises

1. Start a prayer journal. List everything about which you pray and the dates. Note each time you pray about the same thing and record what has changed since the last time you prayed about that. Those changes are faith in action, changing carnal prayers to spiritual ones. Especially note in your prayer journal HOW God answered each prayer as opposed to what you expected.

2. As part of your daily prayer, pray a portion of scripture. Meditate on each verse until it becomes meaningful to you in a practical way. Listen for the voice of the Holy Spirit leading you into truth. Write down what you have learned and list ways to put these truths into practice that same day.

3. Begin making "faith statements". After you have prayed over a need, begin acting as you would if you knew the

answer was on its way. Use wisdom - don't write checks when the money is not in the bank, but practice speaking about the problem as though it were in the process of being solved. Remind yourself each time you feel anxious that in the spirit world, the answer is being worked out and when it is done, it will materialize.

Notes

BREAKING THE ALABASTER BOX

Lesson 4: Teach Me to Pray - Hallowed Be Thy Name

Matthew 6:9 After this manner therefore pray ye: Our
Father which art in heaven, Hallowed be thy name.
10 Thy kingdom come, Thy will be done in earth, as
it is in heaven.
11 Give us this day our daily bread.
12 And forgive us our debts, as we forgive our
debtors.
13 And lead us not into temptation, but deliver us
from evil: For thine is the kingdom, and the power,
and the glory, for ever. Amen.

To "hallow" something means to look at it as holy and sacred. According to Jesus, God's name is already hallowed - in heaven. All the power and majesty of Heaven is invested in one Name: the name Jesus. "Jesus" is the Greek translation of the English transliteration (Joshua) of the Hebrew name "Yeshua", which means "Jehovah My Savior". Although many young men throughout history have been called by that name, only Jesus Christ perfectly embodies its meaning. In Philippians we are told that His is the name above every name. Acts 4:12 tells us that this is the only Name that saves us - the Name of Jesus.

Everything we do as Christians should be done in the Name of Jesus. Prayer is no exception. Most of us end our prayers by saying "In Jesus's Name, Amen". Praying in his name is much more than the closing to our prayers. In fact, it would not hurt to begin our prayers that way because to invoke the Name of Jesus is to invoke his power and authority.

We would have no right to pray, if it were not for Jesus's sacrifice on Calvary. It is his sinless life and atoning blood which provide us the right to the divine relationship. It is all in him. All power and authority is vested in Jesus. Therefore when we pray, we must call upon the Name and plead his blood to gain an audience before the throne.

Thankfully, because we can call upon his Name and the blood has been applied to our lives, we have the right to appear boldly before the throne of Grace. We have been given the gift of the Name and we must use it wisely. To effectively access the power of this Name in prayer, we must keep it hallowed in our heart.

When we are baptized in His Name, we are a part of the Royal Family and we have the authority to use the power of the Name to gain entrance to the throne room. Remember that Heaven is the spirit realm and prayer is our means of crossing into that realm. The power of the Name lies in Heaven, where it carries all authority. The Name of Jesus is a battle cry and our war is spiritual.

Because the Name is so powerful, we must take the greatest care not to misuse it. Taking the Lord's Name in vain is broader than curse words. To flippantly use the Name of Jesus in conversation is like shooting a gun into the air. It is even worse to be casual with this powerful Name in prayer. The Name of Jesus is given to us as a powerful tool in prayer, but we must use it correctly to receive the benefit.

To invoke the Name of Jesus in prayer effectively, we must first know that what we ask is of God. We must learn to align our requests with the manifest will of God - his Word. When we have a confirmed personal application of God's word for our particular situation, then we may speak the Name with boldness and authority.

When we say the Name of Jesus in prayer, we invoke all of Heaven to aid us. When we use the Name we engage in spiritual warfare. Therefore, we don't trivialize it by using it as a ritual, or repeating it for every personal need or prayer request. The power of the Name does not grow with repetition. If we call upon Jesus as we begin to pray , Heaven comes to attention to listen as long as we talk. There is no need to repeat ourselves unless we meet spiritual opposition.

The Name "Jesus" is our greatest weapon in spiritual warfare. We enter into spiritual warfare when we sense in the Spirit that a demonic attack is blocking the answer to our prayer. When God has revealed demonic interference, we immediately call upon His Name. Demons must bow before that Name. At least for a time, they must yield the field.

Sometimes our situation is simply too urgent for eloquent prayer. When the car veers off the road, there is no time for anything but one heartfelt cry. Those are the moments when the Name is the most precious. In our moment of peril, we need only say, "Jesus" and He is there.

Then there are times when we are overwhelmed and don't know how to pray. The Name is knowledge enough. In those moments, we simply cry, "Jesus, fix it." And he does.

When use the Name of Jesus in our prayers, we are claiming intimacy and authority with the Savior. Empowered with the Name, we can come with boldness to lay our petitions before God. Isn't it good to know that we are on a first name basis with our Creator? Thank God you know His Name!

Discussion

1. What is the significance of a name in our relationship with God?
2. What our some ways we can unconsciously misuse the Name?
3. How do we use the Name of Jesus in spiritual warfare?
4. What are specific examples of the authority the Name of Jesus gives us?

Exercises

1. Use your prayer journal to list the most important things you do on an ordinary day. Think about what it means to do those things in the Name of Jesus. How would that change how you see these activities and how you approach them? Are there changes Jesus would want you to make? List those things you feel Jesus would want you to do specifically to be more pleasing to him in your daily life. Pick one change at a time and implement this list in your life. Note in your journal the results.

2, Do a self-check for using the Name of the Lord in vain. Perhaps you do not curse, but are you casual or flippant? Remember we have the right to be intimate with Jesus, but we must always be respectful, as we would with our parents. Ask God to convict you each time you slip and keep a record. Find someone to confess your slips and to share accountability Apologize to God for each slip and say a word of praise and love.

3. List those prayer needs for which you have prayed the longest with no tangible answer. Come boldly into prayer with this list. Call out the Name of Jesus and ask Him to give you a fresh Word from Heaven. Meditate daily on scripture. Write down what God tells you through the Spirit. Repeat daily until the need is met.

Notes

BREAKING THE ALABASTER BOX

Lesson 5: Thy Kingdom Come, Thy Will Be Done Part On Earth As It Is In Heaven1: Kingdom Prayers

Matthew 6:9 After this manner therefore pray ye: Our Father which art in heaven, Hallowed be thy name.
10 Thy kingdom come, Thy will be done in earth, as it is in heaven.
11 Give us this day our daily bread.
12 And forgive us our debts, as we forgive our debtors.
13 And lead us not into temptation, but deliver us from evil: For thine is the kingdom, and the power, and the glory, for ever. Amen.

Jesus instructed us to pray for the coming of the Kingdom. Just what is the Kingdom of God? God's kingdom is his church. Isn't it already here? Do we still have to pray for it's coming?

It is important to remember what we have learned about the spirit realm of Heaven. Things happen first there, before they happen here on the natural level. In Heaven, Jesus is King of Kings and Lord of Lords. But today, Satan is the Prince of this World. Oh, yes, one day, every knee will bow and every tongue confess that Jesus Christ is Lord. That day has not yet come. Therefore, although we are already citizens of that Kingdom, we must still pray for its transfer from Heaven to Earth.

God requires faith to be loosed by humans in prayer for anything he wishes to do here. He does not need our assistance for anything he wishes to do in Heaven; there his will goes forth as soon as he speaks, just as it did on Earth before the fall. Since the enemy of our souls acquired the lease of this planet, God is bound by faith loosed through our words in prayer in order to achieve his will here. For God's Kingdom to come, we must pray.

There are two major areas for which we must pray for the coming of God's kingdom. First, we must pray for the completion of God's divine plan for the human race. We must pray for God to have his way in every nation and in every event of human history. Every natural disaster, every political election, every war and each economic disturbance is used by our Father to bring his Kingdom to Earth. The disasters which take lives and break our hearts are all known to him and though they are created by the Enemy, God uses them as fertilizer for his coming Kingdom. What matters to God must also matter to us.

What do the prayers of one person matter in the face of international heartbreak? One person's fervent prayer can change the world. Intercessory prayer is the most important ministry in which to engage. In fact, intercession is the foundation for every ministry. There is no problem too big for us to make a difference. God counts on us to loose the faith He needs to bring down His manifested will from heaven.

We need organization to help us pray about the big picture which may not touch our daily lives. Some people say they never watch the news or read a newspaper because it is depressing. If we are uninformed about current events, how will we fulfill our role of loosing God's will for mankind into the Earth? We need to seek the information we need in order to fulfill our purpose as intercessors for God's will to be done on Earth as it is in Heaven.

There is no need for great knowledge of the situation, or even great revelation of God's plan. God might choose to reveal things to us, but even if he does not, we can be mightily used in the place of intercessory prayer for the nations. "Lord Jesus, have your way" can be a mighty prayer. Yet the Holy Spirit can help us pray over these overwhelming needs and we can pray powerfully effective prayers.

We can always pray for mercy. We can always pray to restrain evil and protect the innocent. We can pray for God's truth and Spirit to be revealed. And we can pray that Christians will receive guidance on how to best manifest

Jesus in a global situation. But above all, we pray for the Father's will to be manifest on Earth just as it is already manifest in Heaven.

The second area in which we pray for the manifest Will of the Father is in the lives of individuals around us. Everyone put in our paths is there for a purpose. From our families and friends, to the receptionist at the doctor's office, to the stranger we pass on the street. All are sent by God. Everyone around us is ours for the ministry of prayer.

Perhaps we will only be able to pray for a person one time. Perhaps we will pray for them every day for the rest of our lives. Whether one prayer, or many, each prayer for each person looses the will of God into that life by the words of faith. We may only discover the value of our little prayers when we reach Heaven.

Each person we encounter is an opportunity for intercessory prayer. Every need is a chance to release faith. Whether we have no idea of what the person needs or we have prayed for a lost relative for years, no prayer is wasted. Remember that the will of God is already perfected in Heaven and waiting to be set free.

Thus no prayer is ever wasted. Each time we intercede for someone, the will of God is loosed in that individual's life. It does not matter the subject of the prayer. Each intercessory prayer brings a little bit of Heaven to Earth. Every ministry has a foundation of intercessory prayer. Prayer is the greatest act of ministry we can perform.

Praying for others is more than a duty. It is a joy. When we engage in intercessory prayer, we become partners with God in bringing his kingdom from Heaven to Earth. What greater honor could God bestow on us than to allow us to share in his great plan for mankind? Let me pray for someone today!

Discussion

1. What still needs to be revealed on Earth concerning the kingdom of God?

2. Why does God need our prayers?

3. Are only some people called to intercession?

4. How does intercessory prayer help me grow spiritually?

Exercises

`1. Buy a newspaper or watch the evening news for a week. Using your prayer journal, list the international or regional news stories of greatest significance. Pray for these situations.

2. As you meditate on scripture, ask the Lord to reveal his will for our nation in the end times. Each day, boldly pray for this will to be done.

3. Pray for each person who crosses your path each day; loosing the will of God in their lives.

Notes

BREAKING THE ALABASTER BOX

Lesson 6: Thy Kingdom Come, Thy Will Be Done Part On Earth As It Is In Heaven 2: Personal Destiny

Matthew 6:9 After this manner therefore pray ye: Our Father which art in heaven, Hallowed be thy name.
10 Thy kingdom come, Thy will be done in earth, as it is in heaven.
11 Give us this day our daily bread.
12 And forgive us our debts, as we forgive our debtors.
13 And lead us not into temptation, but deliver us from evil: For thine is the kingdom, and the power, and the glory, for ever. Amen.

We have learned that the purpose of prayer is to bring the manifest will of God from Heaven to Earth. Do you realize that before the foundation of the world, God prepared for you a purpose and prepared you for that purpose? Would it surprise you to learn that everyone of us who has the Spirit of God is called of God to a ministry? We loose the perfected will of Heaven into our lives through prayer.

Rom 8:29 For whom he did foreknow, he also did predestinate to be conformed to the image of his Son, that he might be the firstborn among many brethren.

Rom 8:30 Moreover whom he did predestinate, them he also called: and whom he called, them he also justified: and whom he justified, them he also glorified.

God looked down through time to you and me and saw that we

would serve him. So he planned our destiny; he established his will for our lives in heaven. Our Father determined our purpose and established our ministry before the foundation of the world.

God put this call upon our lives, this summons to service if you will, even before we knew him. God drew us to him in order to loose our destiny in our lives. When we achieve our purpose, the glory of our destiny, perfected in heaven, will appear in our lives.

Once we understand that God has planted a destiny within each of us, it is our job to first determine that destiny and then loose that destiny. Both are accomplished through prayer.

How do we discover our personal ministry, which is our reason for living, our purpose, our mission, our destiny? First, we take our talents, our dreams, and our successes to God in prayer. We ask God to anoint the things which give us joy. We consecrate our talents to his glory rather than our own.

Then we act upon that about which we first prayed. As we pray for more specific revelation about our destiny, we put into practice what we already know. As we grow in knowledge of the Word, knowledge of ourselves, and prayer, we grow into our destiny.

God reveals our destiny to us in stages, but he knows the end from the beginning. Step by step, he prepares us for our future. This is why we should talk to God about his plans for us on a regular basis. We will map our destiny one revelation at a time.

As we grow into our future, we understand better how to pray about it. As God's purpose is unfolded around us, we become partners with God in achieving our destiny. The more we see confirmation of our calling in our lives, the higher our faith rises. The higher our faith rises, the more powerfully we pray.

Another reason praying about our ministry and purpose is important is to gain confirmation of the will of God. Remember, we are releasing the heavenly will of God to be manifested in our earthly lives. While God will use the talents and interests which he gives us, our ultimate purpose is for God to choose. Our path to purpose may not take the direction we expect or the direction which we would choose it the choice were ours to make. In order to reach our destiny and fulfill our purpose, we must pray for God's will to be done and not ours.

As we pray, God prepares us for the future and moves us forward. Through our prayers of faith, we loose purpose into our life and the destiny God has prepared for us in heaven is manifested on Earth. Nothing but our lack of faith and failure to pray can prevent our predestined purpose from coming to pass.

It is exciting to learn that God has a divine plan and purpose for our life. Through prayer, we can loose what is already in place in Heaven to be manifested here on Earth. Pray for your destiny today.

Discussion

1. How do we find the will of God for our lives?

2. Where is the first place to look in our search for our purpose?

3. What are your thoughts about why God reveals our destiny in stages?

Exercises

1. Write a list of all your gifts, talents and interests. Lift the list up before God and make an offering of all of them for His purposes.

2. Pray to know and use your spiritual Gifts. Ask God to anoint you for ministry and use you in his kingdom.

3. If you are not engaged in ministry, pray for guidance and find a ministry. If you are engaged in ministry, pray for the anointing daily.

4. Ask God to manifest his purpose for your life and lead you to your destiny.

5. Record in your prayer journal each revelation about your purpose and when it comes to pass.

Notes

BREAKING THE ALABASTER BOX

Lesson 7:Give Us This Day Our Daily Bread

Matthew 6:9 After this manner therefore pray ye: Our
Father which art in heaven, Hallowed be thy name.
10 Thy kingdom come, Thy will be done in earth, as
it is in heaven.
11 Give us this day our daily bread.
12 And forgive us our debts, as we forgive our
debtors.
13 And lead us not into temptation, but deliver us
from evil: For thine is the kingdom, and the power,
and the glory, for ever. Amen.

There is a secret to having peace in the face of need. With one application of divine principle, we can sweep away fear and anxiety. We know God has promised to care for us; we also know how overwhelming life can be at times. In those overwhelming times, we can claim our promised provision and peace by praying the principle "One Day At A Time".

The principle was illustrated in the manna which fell fresh every morning. There could be no hoarding; hoarding would be a lack of faith; doubting that the next day's manna would fall. There could be no lazy failure to obey, for that would mean going hungry. To be fed required faith - trust and obedience. So it is today. We trust and obey for each day's provision. Give us this day our daily bread.

The secret is as simple as that. Each day, when we pray, we ask for what we need that day. We expect to receive what we need for that day. We do not worry about the future; we rest on the promise that we will receive new grace for each new day.

To have faith to pray for today's needs means that I must be clear about what I really need today. I particularly remember one day several years ago as I brought my needs to God. I told him, "Father, my rent is due in two weeks and I have no money. My electric bill is due in ten days and I have no money. My phone bill is due in five days and I have no money. What am I going to do?" God replied, "Do you have a roof over your head and food today?" "Yes", I replied. "Do you have a phone and lights today?" "Yes." "Then", God told me gently, "Wait until I let you down to complain." When the due date came for each bill, the money was there. And I learned how to pray for my daily bread.

Of course, we must sometimes consider the future. Sensible people must plan ahead. Sometimes it takes much prayer to develop the faith to loose our answer. It is never wrong to pray about what concerns us, God is interested in our future, as well as our present. But faith is the key to the answer and "daily" is the key to faith.

We may safely leave all our cares and troubles in God's lap in prayer. The secret is to leave them there. Once we have cast our cares upon him, we should not take them back again. We will not be discouraged if the answer does not come today; we look for the results that belong to today. We confidently expect our daily bread.

Expectation causes us to look for the promised blessing for today. In his example prayer, Jesus assured us of the existence of daily blessings. Each day we loose today's blessings with today's faith. Sometimes we spend so much time worrying about tomorrow that we miss what God is doing for us today. We need to locate today's blessings and in our prayers offer thanks. By so doing, we raise our level of faith in preparation for tomorrow's blessings.

Living and praying in the present brings us peace. We can leave our long term problems in God's hands and look for today's answers. We can increase our faith and see the results of our prayers. One day at a time.

Discussion

1. What are some reasons for only receiving God's provision one day at a time?

2. How can I use the principle of daily provision to lift my faith today?

Exercises

1. Look back at your Prayer Journal, where in Lesson 3 you began recording your requests and your faith journey for each one. Note the date when each was answered and look for the timing with which God answers our prayers. Try to discover how to tell when God is about to move in a particular situation; in other words, when that need becomes "today's bread".

2. Just before bedtime today, think about and write down every blessing you have received, small and great. These blessings are your "daily bread".

3. Each time you feel anxiety over an unmet need, pray for peace. Peace can be our answer for today.

Notes

BREAKING THE ALABASTER BOX

Lesson 8: Forgive Our Debts As We Forgive Our Debtors

Matthew 6:9 After this manner therefore pray ye: Our Father which art in heaven, hallowed be thy name.

10 Thy kingdom come, Thy will be done in earth, as it is in heaven.

11 Give us this day our daily bread.

12 And forgive us our debts, as we forgive our debtors.

13 And lead us not into temptation, but deliver us from evil: For thine is the kingdom, and the power, and the glory, for ever. Amen.

Nothing interferes with our relationship to God like sin and bitterness. Therefore, repentance and forgiveness are a regular, daily part of our prayer life. We need to clear the lines of communication each day so that unrepented sin and unforgiveness of others do not hinder the answers we need.

It is important to forgive and repent at the same time in prayer, because repentance and forgiveness are intertwined. Scripture teaches us that unless we forgive, we will not be forgiven. Unless we show mercy, we will not receive mercy. Since none of us can do without mercy, we must release any grudge against others that is in our heart before our repentance will be received.

Connecting repentance and forgiveness makes both easier for us. How much easier it is to let go of bitterness towards others who do not perhaps deserve it, if I realize that by doing so, I gain mercy for myself.! How much easier it is to repent with the understanding that I am not alone in needing mercy. So each time I pray, I repent and forgive; releasing the mercy of God into my heart and into my life.

Whether we repent and forgive first thing every day when we pray, or whether we repent and forgive as soon as we realize the need, we must be diligent to do both daily. The longer we wait to repent or forgive, the harder it becomes as our heart becomes harder. After a period of time, a root of bitterness springs up, blocking the Spirit of God and hindering our relationship with Him. If we find our prayers becoming ineffective, we need to check for unrepented sin and unforgiveness in our hearts.

As we sit in God's presence, we ask him to show us sin and bitterness in our heart which may not even be known to us. The Holy Spirit searches us and reveals what we need to repent and forgive. When we speak the words, grace is loosed and the lines of communication are reopened.

Of course, there is more to repentance and forgiveness than merely reciting words. Just expressing the willingness does not immediately produce the results. Yet merely speaking the words releases grace to help us achieve true repentant and forgiving actions. It is not possible to pray for someone regularly and still harbor resentment. In the same way, regularly expressing sorrow over sin and meaning it prepares the soil of our character to be changed with the Fruit of the Spirit.

If unforgiveness toward others costs us forgiveness for own our sins, the opposite is also true. When we show mercy, we receive mercy. Praying for those who seem to least deserve it causes God to view our inadequacies through the lens of grace.

Repentance and forgiveness are like a daily spiritual bath. Through them, we cleanse our heart and maintain our souls as a vessel of the Holy Spirit. Through them we claim intimacy with the Father. Rather than viewing repentance and forgiveness as unpleasant obligations, we should see them as the means to spiritual renewal and new life.
I don't want to miss my daily spiritual bath!

Discussion

1. How have sin an unforgiveness hindered

your prayers in the past?
2. How can unforgiveness affect us without our awareness?
3. What are some ways we can practice forgiveness?

Exercises

1. Ask God to reveal those things in your life which are a
barrier between you and Him. Write these things in your journal and
repent of them daily until you are delivered.

2. Ask God to reveal any person against whom you hold bitterness
or unforgiveness in your heart. State your willingness to forgive
and pray for these people regularly.

3. Be sure to revisit your journal pages and leave space to
record your victories in repentance and forgiveness.

Notes

BREAKING THE ALABASTER BOX

Lesson 9: Lead Us Not Into Temptation, But Deliver Us From Evil.

Matthew 6:9 After this manner therefore pray ye:
Our Father which art
in heaven, Hallowed be thy name.
10 Thy kingdom come, Thy will be done in earth, as
it is in heaven.
11 Give us this day our daily bread.
12 And forgive us our debts, as we forgive our
debtors.
13 And lead us not into temptation, but deliver us
from evil: For
thine is the kingdom, and the power, and the glory,
for ever. Amen.

God alone controls our future. We don't know and cannot see what the future holds. Some people live in fear of what might be around the next corner in their life. As children of God, we need not fear the unknown future. By loosing prayers of faith, we can be led fearlessly into whatever lies ahead, confident of the protection and leadership of Jesus.

Of course, God is not going to detour us around all trouble and trials. He sends us some difficulty to help us grow. However, lack of direction causes unnecessary suffering and hardship. If we pray about our future, we can receive direction and thus protection.

First, we are to pray not to be led into temptation. That might seem a strange prayer, since we know God tempts no one. The devil uses our human weaknesses to deceive us. From that deception comes our temptations. In order to steer us away from temptation, God must lead us into truth.

When we pray for truth, we are praying for two things. First, we are praying for revelation. We are asking God to help us understand the scriptures and what he requires of us. Knowledge is the first line of defense against temptation.

When temptation comes, we can defeat it with the Word. Jesus used the Word to defeat temptation. Jesus used the Word to confound the devil and strengthen himself. When we pray scripture, we loose the power of the Word against the enemy. By giving us the Word, God leads us away from temptation.

Secondly, when God gives us revelation, he gives us wisdom. The Holy Spirit takes the word and implants it in our hearts; making it a part of our everyday life. The wisdom of the Word is a shield against temptation, because with wisdom, we know how to fight. With his wisdom, Jesus leads us away from temptation and leads us into the light.

We can also protect ourselves by asking Jesus to deliver us from evil. Remember that prayer looses faith into the spiritual realm to bring God's will to earth. God wants to direct our paths but we must ask him.
Before we make a decision, we must ask him. God knows the pitfalls inherent along any path we choose.

Each time we pray, we not only ask God about specific issues and decisions which we may be facing, but we surrender afresh our lives to his direction. When we renew our commitment to obedience in our daily prayers, we place our future in the only secure place: the center of God's will.

God protects us from many dangers of which we are never aware. We cannot count the accidents which did not happen or the sickness that never came. We can, however, spare ourselves much suffering by asking God to save us from what we cannot see. By faith, we can be secure in the path we walk, knowing that our faith has loosed the protective power of God into our lives.

When we pray, we should pray with an open Bible, asking for revelation which will help us avoid temptation. We should always place our future, through prayer, into the hands of our Heavenly Father who will protect us from the unseen. Daily we should invoke the protection of God which enables us to resist temptation and delivers us from evil.

Discussion

1. How are we protected from temptations by God's Word?
2. How has God protected you from harm you could not see coming?

Excercises

1. As you meditate upon scripture in your daily prayer time, note the practical applications of the passage and try to apply them that day. Write this in your journal so you can record your progress in this area.

2. Ask God to reveal areas in your life which are sources of temptation. Pray for wisdom to escape the traps of Satan.

3. Make a list of things that might happen in the future of which you are afraid. Do not record them in your journal. Pray over this list and place control of your future completely in God's hands. Then tear up the list.

Notes

BREAKING THE ALABASTER BOX

Lesson 10: For Thine is the Kingdom

Matthew 6:9 After this manner therefore pray ye: Our
Father which art in heaven, Hallowed be thy name.
10 Thy kingdom come, Thy will be done in earth, as
it is in heaven.
11 Give us this day our daily bread.
12 And forgive us our debts, as we forgive our
debtors.
13 And lead us not into temptation, but deliver us
from evil: For thine is the kingdom, and the power,
and the glory, for ever. Amen.

Praise and thanksgiving should always be a part of our prayer life. As much as God has done for us, spontaneous and heartfelt praise should come easily to us. Sometimes, however, the words simply fail us. Jesus, in this model prayer helps us to find the words to express our heart by giving us four categories of praise.

The first category of praise is to acknowledge God's authority and rule: For thine is the kingdom. Jesus is our king. As our king, Jesus has all authority in in our lives. His Word is our chief delight. His will our ambition. The kingship of Jesus in our lives is not oppressive. Because he is Lord of every situation, we do not have to find our own way or devise our own plan. That is reason to praise him!

During our daily prayer time, we can call Jesus "King", "Majesty", "Sovereign". We can thank him for being ruler of our lives and doing all things well. We can bow before his authority and declare our willingness to obey and serve him. With joy, we can sing to him, "He's my King and oh I dearly love him".

We also praise God for his power. All power, perfect power belongs to him. There is no problem too difficult for God to handle. The Creator of the universe has all resource at his disposal. Our Father need only speak and worlds are brought into existence or destroyed. He needs no army to enforce his will.

We should thank God every day for his power manifested in our life. Every need met can be turned to praise of God's power. Even making requests is a form of praise, because asking God to move in our life displays faith in his power. The greatest compliment we can pay to the power of God is by submitting to God's will and allowing that power to change our lives. But he longs to hear us thank him and praise him for all the powerful things he has done for us.

To God belongs all the glory. Glory: majesty, honor, prestige, deference, respect. God is worthy of them all. In fact, God is the only one worthy of glory in all the universe. Every human achievement is the result of God's inspiration. As the Creator, God's glory and might are always on display. Every day, we should look for God's glory in our life, because the glory of God conveys purpose, peace and joy.

God's glory is easier to praise than his authority of power. God's glory is simply beautiful. Then again, God's glory is so beautiful, words fail us. But as we grasp to express our awe of God's glory, it helps to remember those moments of the day when we felt that awe. Sharing them with our Father, thanking him for revealing his glory to us, warms his heart. God wants to hear how much we enjoyed that beautiful sunrise. And the more we praise him for his glory, the more of his glory God will reveal to us.

God especially deserves our praise because he is. Always. Forever. He is the Ancient of Days. God always has been and forever shall be. What a reason to praise him!

The best way to show praise for the eternity of our God is to trust him with our own eternity. To choose to follow him, believing his promises of eternal life, is the best praise we could shower on our Heavenly Father. We should renew that commitment each day in prayer by declaring our trust in him. We should thank him for heaven, where we will live forever with him. We should praise him for granting eternity to us.

Words may fail us, but our hearts are full. Every day we can lift a new song of praise to God for his kingdom, power, glory and eternity. The more we pray, the more we praise.

Discussion

1. How is the authority of Jesus a source of praise in our lives?
2. How do we best trust God for his power?
3. How is God glorious to you?
4. Describe eternity.

Exercises

1. In your prayer journal, list all the benefits you have received from being a Child of God. Tell God how much you appreciate these blessings.

2. What are some needs in your life which God has met with supernatural power? Thank him again for all of them.

3. Take a walk around your yard and look closely at the intricate design of nature. Write a poem about how nature reveals God's glory.

4. Tell God what you are looking forward to about Heaven.

Notes

BREAKING THE ALABASTAR BOX LESSON ELEVEN

Prayer Warriors of the Word - Abraham

We have looked together at the components of prayer which Jesus taught in the model prayer. We have learned a lot in these lessons about how effective prayer works. Now let's look at some great prayer warriors of the Bible, who can illustrate for us how to put prayer principles into practice.

ABRAHAM

Gen. 18:22 And the men turned their faces from
thence, and went toward Sodom: but Abraham
stood yet before the LORD.
23 And Abraham drew near, and said, Wilt thou
also destroy the righteous with the wicked?
24 Peradventure there be fifty righteous within the
city: wilt thou also destroy and not spare the place
for the fifty righteous that are therein?
25 That be far from thee to do after this manner, to
slay the righteous with the wicked: and that the
righteous should be as the wicked, that be far from
thee: Shall not the Judge of all the earth do right?
26 And the LORD said, If I find in Sodom fifty
righteous within the city, then I will spare all the
place for their sakes.
27 And Abraham answered and said, Behold now, I
have taken upon me to speak unto the LORD, which
am but dust and ashes:
28 Peradventure there shall lack five of the fifty
righteous: wilt thou destroy all the city for lack of
five? And he said, If I find there forty and five, I
will not destroy it.
29 And he spake unto him yet again, and said,
Peradventure there shall be forty found there. And

he said, I will not do it for forty's sake.
30 And he said unto him, Oh let not the LORD be
angry, and I will speak: Peradventure there shall
thirty be found there. And he said, I will not do it, if
I find thirty there.
31 And he said, Behold now, I have taken upon me
to speak unto the LORD: Peradventure there shall
be twenty found there. And he said, I will not
destroy it for twenty's sake.
32 And he said, Oh let not the LORD be angry, and
I will speak yet but this once: Peradventure ten shall
be found there. And he said, I will not destroy it for
ten's sake.

God had brought his servant Abraham word of his plan to destroy sinful Sodom. Abraham understood the reason for the revelation; the reason was intercession. God shared with Abraham the coming judgment of Sodom in order that Abraham could intervene and loose the faith that could change God's mind.

Abraham was especially interested in Sodom because his nephew Lot and family lived there. Because of his personal interest, Abraham felt a spiritual burden for the whole city. Armed with God's revelations about the future of Sodom, Abraham went to work as an intercessor.

Because Abraham understood the reason for the revelation, he could enter into intercession boldly. Abraham asks God a question to which he already knows the answer. "Will you punish the innocent with the guilty?"

That almost sounds impudent, but Abraham had to base his intercession on the revealed nature and will of God for it to succeed. Abraham knew that God is ever just. Therefore, Abraham knew that God would demonstrate that justice by delivering any innocent people living in Sodom. Like Lot.

Lot had made an unwise choice in moving to Sodom, but he was a righteous man. Abraham was confident that a just God would spare Lot and any righteous left with him in that depraved city. Armed with the faith that knowing God can bring, Abraham began to intercede.

What if there were 50 righteous souls in that wicked city? Or 40? Abraham exhausted his boldness when he exhausted his faith at the number "10". And God agreed.

But there were not 10 righteous souls in Sodom. Not even 10. Basically, there was Lot and his wife and two rather doubtful daughters. So Abraham's intercession failed. Or did it?

Sodom was destroyed just as God had planned. But Lot and his daughters were spared by angelic intervention. Abraham's persistence had changed God's mind. That is why Abraham is a role model for prayer.

Persistence, to be effective, must be based on faith. We must absolutely KNOW that we are praying the will of God. In order to have that certainty, we must have a word from God revealing his will. God's revelation to us is two-fold. God's Word is Logos and Rhema.

God's Logos Word is the written word, the Bible. The foundation of all revealed will of God is the scripture. When we wish to intercede and pray the will of God, we start with scripture. What does the Bible say about our need? Scripture will provide the general principles which will guide our inspiration.

The Rhema is the personal word which the Holy Spirit speaks to us in prayer. Many things can affect our understanding of the Holy Spirit when he speaks. Therefore, always check your Rhema against the Bible and pray for an outside confirmation. Now you are ready to intercede.

Armed with the knowledge of God's will, it is possible to be bold in prayer. We can be bold in persistence; we can keep asking until our petition is granted. We can also be bold by being specific. Rather than simply ask for healing for a headache, seek to discover and permanently heal the high blood pressure causing the headaches. We can pray for a car with air conditioning and good gas mileage. We can pray boldly because God has revealed his will to us.
So, for powerful intercession, we first seek God's will in a matter. Then we pray persistently and specifically. With boldness we intercede and lives are changed. We can be Abrahams today.

Discussion

1, How do we determine God's will in any specific situation?
2. What role does the Holy Spirit play in determining God's specific will?

3. How does praying specifically empower our prayers?

Exercises

1. Write down the greatest need of another person in your life of which you are aware. Pray for one week to seek God's will for that person and their need. Write down the insights which you receive.

2. Do a Bible study on the subject of the need. Record what you learn.

3. Go into the presence of God with this need with boldness. Pray specifically and pray persistently until the need is met.

Notes

Breaking the Alabaster Box - Lesson 12

Prayer Warriors of the Word - Moses

Num. 14:11 And the LORD said unto Moses, How long will this people provoke me? and how long will it be ere they believe me, for all the signs which I have showed among them?

12 I will smite them with the pestilence, and disinherit them, and will make of thee a greater nation and mightier than they.

13 And Moses said unto the LORD, Then the Egyptians shall hear it, (for thou broughtest up this people in thy might from among them;)

14 And they will tell it to the inhabitants of this land: for they have heard that thou LORD art among this people, that thou LORD art seen face to face, and that thy cloud standeth over them, and that thou goest before them, by day time in a pillar of a cloud, and in a pillar of fire by night.

15 Now if thou shalt kill all this people as one man, then the nations which have heard the fame of thee will speak, saying,

16 Because the LORD was not able to bring this people into the land which he sware unto them, therefore he hath slain them in the wilderness.

Like Abraham, Moses was a great intercessor, but Moses was not praying to save his family. He was praying to save people who were not being nice to him at all. In fact, God's anger and decision to destroy Israel stemmed from their rebellion against the authority of Moses. God planned to start over and use Moses to create a more righteous nation, more worthy of blessing. Why would Moses turn down an offer like that? Because Moses understood that prayer and ministry are always about mercy.

If we understand our place in the prayer line of communication, we can be much more effective in intercession. The role of an intercessor is always to be the looser of mercy into lives which need it . Intercession is the reason God reveals his intentions to us. Mercy is the reason behind every intercession.

Think about it for a moment. God did not need Moses to ask him to destroy Israel. God had the power and God had the plan. But God needed faith to loose mercy into the situation; God must have faith in order to do anything but judge this planet. God needs intercessors of mercy and he is calling us to intercede where we are most needed.

No matter what else our calling, we are all called to be intercessors. Intercessors are always vessels of mercy. When we pray, we seek to loose God's mercy in our life and into the lives of others. By so doing, we gain the mercy which we need.

The ultimate mission of intercessory prayer is to pray for our enemies as Moses did. When we pray for our enemies to receive mercy, we will accomplish one of the most difficult tasks we will ever attempt. When we pray for mercy, we can feel mercy. When we feel mercy, we can receive mercy.

Just how do we manage to pray sincerely for those who have wronged and hurt us? We first acknowledge to ourselves and God that we have hurt and wronged others and that we need mercy too. Asking God to forgive us for our resentment towards the person for whom we are about to pray, looses mercy and anointing into our lives, preparing us to intercede.

Then we invoke the Golden Rule. We pray, not as our nemesis deserves, but as we would want for ourselves to be treated. We pray for them all the blessings which we want for ourselves. We pray for our enemies as though we loved them and in so doing, we come to love them. The best way to lose an enemy is to pray for him.

Something powerful happens when we pray for an enemy. The power of mercy is released into their life and ours. Forgiveness becomes a reality. Relationships are restored. The burden of resentment is lifted forever. If your prayer life has been sluggish, schedule some time to pray for your worst enemy today.

Discussion

1. What is the role of an intercessor in prayer?

2. How does interceding for our enemies bless us?

3. What role does forgiveness play in intercession?

Exercises

1. Ask God to reveal to you any person against whom you have resentment. Write these names in your prayer journal.

2. Ask God to forgive you for the resentment you bear these people. Release your resentment to God.

3. Intercede for these people, asking God to bless them in every area of their life, particularly in the area where they offended you.

Notes

I Sam. 1:9 So Hannah rose up after they had eaten in Shiloh, and after they had drunk. Now Eli the priest sat upon a seat by a post of the temple of the LORD.

10 And she was in bitterness of soul, and prayed unto the LORD, and wept sore.

11 And she vowed a vow, and said, O LORD of hosts, if thou wilt indeed look on the affliction of thine handmaid, and remember me, and not forget thine handmaid, but wilt give unto thine handmaid a man child, then I will give him unto the LORD all the days of his life, and there shall no razor come upon his head.

Hannah wanted a child more than anything else in the world. In the natural order of things, it wasn't happening. This unfulfilled desire had leached all the joy out of Hannah's life; all she felt was bitter gall. But Hannah did not allow her despair to embitter her heart towards God. Hannah made the only decision a woman of prayer could make. She took her pain to God.

Being vulnerable and honest in the presence of God is the first crucial element of petition. God knows our hearts, but he wants us to willingly share our inner selves with him. God can see when we are angry or impatient with him. When we willingly acknowledge our doubt and pain, then faith is loosed in that painful situation.

Our Father is moved by our pain, which is an excellent reason to share that pain with him. Hezekiah's tears moved God to change his mind and grant him 15 more years of life. God will be a truly loving parent and choose what is best for us, even when it causes us pain. Yet, whenever he can do so without harm to us, God will choose the path of least pain when we entrust our pain to him. Therefore, to simply share with our God our frustrations, pains, and sorrows is an effective form of prayer.

But Hannah did more than express a wish. She presented a proposition to the Father. Give me the desire of my heart and I will give it back to you. What a radical idea! Yet that is exactly what Hannah did; she gave Samuel back to God and left him at the temple when he was only a toddler. She saw her son only once a year to bring him replacements for the clothes which he had outgrown.

Why would anyone want to make such a sacrifice? Because what is dedicated to God is sanctified by God. In other words, when a matter is given to God, the matter becomes God's business. When God gets the glory, the job gets done. Therefore, if you really want your petition to be granted, give Him the glory.

I remember when I was a baby Christian. God had delivered me from many kinds of serious bondage. My life was clean, but rather Spartan. I lived in a shabby efficiency apartment with minimal, secondhand furniture and not so much as a poster on the walls. I asked God to bless me financially, particularly by giving me nicer things - furniture and curtains and nice decorations for my walls. I promised God that if he gave me these things that they would not become a stumbling block or an idol in my life. I promised to bless others with what God blessed me.

You need only take a glance at my home to see that God kept his end of the bargain. My home is only a trailer, but it is cheerful and bright. Each time I give something away, I know I am sanctifying my pretty little home. God can trust me to give, so he can bless me.

This is the attitude Hannah took to prayer. If her petition glorified God, God would glorify her with an answer. This is the way God always works. Show him you can be trusted and you will get your answer!

When you carry your petition to the Lord, send it with a promise! Dedicate the blessing you are seeking to the glory and benefit of God. By doing so, you are sanctifying your petition.

God does not REQUIRE this to answer prayer, but what a marvelous way to honor and trust him! How exciting to become partners with God, aligning his agenda and your petition! Simply by giving it all to God, we can become a Hannah in prayer.

Discussion

1. Does God need anything from us to answer our prayer? If so, what?

2. How does dedicating our answered prayers to God's glory bless us?

3. Why would we want to surrender our deepest desires to God?

Exercises

1. Write down the need for which you have been praying the longest.

2. List 3 ways you could minister to others if this need were met.

3. Take this need to God and dedicate the benefits to his glory.

Notes

BREAKING THE ALABASTAR BOX

Lesson 14 - Prayer Warriors of the Word - Cornelius

Acts 10:1 There was a certain man in Caesarea called Cornelius, a centurion of the band called the Italian band,

2 A devout man, and one that feared God with all his house, which gave much alms to the people, and prayed to God alway.

3 He saw in a vision evidently about the ninth hour of the day an angel of God coming in to him, and saying unto him, Cornelius.

4 And when he looked on him, he was afraid, and said, What is it, Lord? And he said unto him, Thy prayers and thine alms are come up for a memorial before God.

Cornelius was looking for an answer. Wisely, Cornelius looked for this answer, not to the Roman government, or Roman gods, but Cornelius looked to Jehovah. Cornelius chose to pray in order to find salvation. Good choice, Cornelius!!

Cornelius was wise not only in the source of his search for answers, but in his methods. Cornelius did not just pray for revelation; he lived the revelation he had. Cornelius demonstrated his sincerity by his behavior. In so doing, he was not attempting to earn an answer or bribe God. Cornelius's almsgiving was actually a form of prayer, another way of reaching after God. Cornelius added faith to his prayer by adding action to his prayer. And that got the attention of God.

Cornelius made a lifestyle of seeking God. Every bit of his strength and focus went into this relationship. He was wise enough to know he needed to know something more. That acknowledged hunger drove Cornelius. The unrelenting hunger brought results. Supernatural results.

Cornelius's determination got the attention of heaven. An angel sent him to Peter and Peter led him and his household to the salvation experience. Because when we live what we pray, God notices and responds.

Are you hungry for more of God? Have you been crying out to God in prayer? Get the attention of Heaven. As an act of faith, begin to live as though you already had that for which you are looking. Change your lifestyle. And keep on praying.

By adding action to your prayers, you will demonstrate powerful faith; faith is what releases God's power into our situation. By giving to others when we are searching for answers touches the heart of God.

So, how do we get started? Let's look at the petition for which we are praying. Perhaps you need a financial blessing. Bless someone financially - tip that mediocre waitress 20 percent. You see, that is ministry and ministry gets God's attention.

Perhaps you are struggling with a habit you cannot seem to break. Forgive a difficult, unrepentant person in your life. When you show mercy, you receive mercy.

Perhaps you just want to grow closer to God. As you pray for deeper understanding of God's Word, repent of disobedience of some area where you understand, but fall short. Recommit to obedience and loose a fresh anointing.

By combining action with your prayers, you demonstrate faith in a tangible way. More faith means quicker answers. You can be a Cornelius today!

Discussion

1. What is the connection between faith and works?

2. How does obedience help us understand the Word?

3. How does obedience help us grow closer to God?

Exercises

1. In your prayer journal, make a list of your most urgent prayer needs. Note how long you have been praying for these petitions.

2. For each unanswered petition, locate a verse of scripture which applies to your need in which you could improve on obedience.

3. Make and record a plan of action which moves you forward in faith in that area.

4. Record the answered prayers, because they are comig!

Notes

BREAKING THE ALABASTAR BOX LESSON 15

Prayer Warriors of the Word - Jesus

Matt. 26:39 And he went a little farther, and fell on his face, and prayed, saying, O my Father, if it be possible, let this cup pass from me: nevertheless not as I will, but as thou wilt.

Jesus is the ultimate prayer warrior! There are many excellent examples of how to pray by imitating our Lord, but this prayer always excites me. I get excited when I hear Jesus asking his Father to spare him the Cross. I get excited because Jesus is proof that I can ask God for anything.

Jesus had to know that his Father could not grant this request. After all, he was born to die for us. Yet he asked anyway. Why? Because Jesus knew the Father would understand!

I can go to my Heavenly Father and share my true and honest feelings without fear of condemnation. In fact, that is what God longs for me to do! Effective prayer which imitates our Lord in prayer demands that I bare my soul in honest self expression when I pray!

But isn't it a sin to be mad at God? Isn't it blasphemy to tell him we don't want to do what he has asked us? Let me ask you something - doesn't God see your mind and your heart? Doesn't he already know? There is a tremendous difference between whining and complaining, which is rebellion and coming with honesty into His presence.

God longs for intimacy with his children. Intimacy requires honesty. As the prayer in the garden shows, we can tell our Father anything! And that is just what he wants us to do!

But why bother praying when you feel the answer will be "no"? First of all, because faith is based upon the Word and will of God. One of the reasons our prayers are not always answered the first time we pray is because we must seek God's will and align our will with it before we can truly release our faith. So take every petition boldly, confident that if your plan needs refining, God will help you with the process.

Another reason to ask when you feel pretty sure the answer is "no" is to ask God's help in accepting his will. This is surely Jesus's purpose in asking to be exempted from the cross. That's why, at the end of the request, Jesus said, "Not my will, but thine be done". There is something about surrendering my will that brings peace, because the matter is now in the Father's hands.

Just expressing our emotions can be beneficial. Simply having Someone listen who cares relieves our load. Our Heavenly Father is the perfect confidante. He will not condemn us for our feelings. In fact, God is more merciful and more trustworthy than humans; he is the safest refuge for our troubles. How wonderful it I indeed that we can tell him anything!

Wonderfully, God can correct any praying amiss that we might do. Grace covers stupid praying. In fact the only stupid praying is the praying you do not do. There is nothing freer, more liberating than being totally honest in the presence of the Lord.

When Jesus prayed for his cup to pass from him, he was engaging in an intimate moment in a real and dynamic relationship with his Father. Jesus could reveal his dread of the cross with no fear of rejection because he surrendered his will to the Father.

Because of Jesus's sacrifice, we can have the same relationship with him. We can bare the hidden places of our hearts and remain confident of his love. We can trust God to correct our thinking and guide us into more effective prayers. And who knows? God often grants requests that we believe he will not grant.

There is no need to hold back with God. Tell him how you really feel today!

Discussion

1. What is the difference between rebellion and honesty in prayer?

2. What are some benefits to praying when the answer is probably “no”?

3. How does Grace cover us when we pray “stupid prayers”?

Exercises

1. In your prayer journal, list all the doubts, fears and rebellious feelings hidden in your heart.

2. Go to God in prayer for each item on the list. Tell your Father how you REALLY feel about these issues. Don’t rush the process. Spend some quality time being honest with the Lord.

3. When you have finished the list (a thorough job may take more than one session of prayer) pray “Thy will be done” and leave your feelings in the hands of the Lord.

4. Be listening - God is going to speak to your circumstances and change them or you - probably both!!

Notes

BREAKING THE ALABASTAR BOX: LESSON 16

Prayer Tips and Tools - Meditation

Josh 1:8 This book of the law shall not depart out of thy mouth; but thou shalt meditate therein day and night, that thou mayest observe to do according to all that is written therein: for then thou shalt make thy way prosperous, and then thou shalt have good success.

The word "meditation" describes perfectly intimate and powerful prayer. Meditation is the listening part of prayer. Listening is the most important part of prayer, as well as the most difficult. Sadly, most Christians spend less time listening than any other part of prayer. When we fail to listen, our prayers become mere laundry lists of complaints. But when we learn to meditate upon the Word of the Lord, our prayer time becomes sweet intimate fellowship with Him.

One of the most difficult aspects of meditation is learning to focus. When we can focus, we can filter out distractions and hear the voice of the Holy Spirit more clearly. Recognizing when the Holy Spirit is speaking to us is much simpler when we hear no other voices but His.

The best tool for meditation is scripture itself. When we open the Bible, God is directly speaking to us. Meditating on the Word during prayer is the best way to focus on the Holy Spirit. Meditation on scripture can deepen our understanding of the Word, as well as allow the Word to speak to our current situation. However, we must be careful not to twist the meaning of scripture to make it say what we want to hear.

I always begin by thinking about the meaning of the scripture in its original context. This focuses my mind and spirit. As I think on the scripture, the small voice of the Spirit brings insights to my mind. I never cease to be amazed at how God can speak to my circumstances from any passage of scripture. Of course, I always seek confirmation to make sure I have heard the Lord correctly.

I meditate on a chapter of scripture daily as part of my devotional time. I pray over one verse of scripture at a time, working my way through the Bible, alternating Old and New Testaments. Praying the Word is a great way to study the Word. In prayer, the Holy Spirit is right beside me, granting me understanding. Praying the Word takes prayer and Bible study to a higher level.

The Word is a must for meditation; but there are other tools as well. I like to use Christian books or devotionals during my meditation time. I find that God can speak even when I disagree with the author! Meditating on these books helps embed the things which I learn from them more deeply in my mind.

I enjoy using tapes of sermons during my time of meditation. Many times I have heard these sermons before, but I seem to get more out of them when I meditate over them. Using these sermon tapes in my prayer time has taught me how to hear the words of the Spirit coming from the lips of a man.

As part of my prayer time, I use praise and worship tapes to help me lift up my Savior. Both tapes and a hymn book are useful praise and worship tools. I even read the hymns to which I do not know the words. When I cannot find the words to express my love for my Savior, these resources can assist me.

So, you see, there are many resources to aid in prayerful meditation. Prayer is our individual daily fellowship with Jesus, we each have to find the tools that best help us. If a resource does not help you hear from God, then use another. God will help you; all you have to do is ask.

One final note of caution. In order to be spiritually safe, it is important to focus upon Jesus. Chanting, or so-called "contemplative prayer" where intense focus happens with a blank mind, are extremely dangerous. It is important to allow only one Spirit to influence our mind. Always focus on scripture or at least on Christian content. To sit with a blank open mind in meditation is to invite contact with the fallen third of the spirit realm. We wish only to hear from the Holy Spirit.

Meditation is simply the art of listening for God's voice. There are many ways to meditate, and you will discover your own tools. The important thing is to listen; hearing from God is the most important part of prayer. True prayer is a two-way conversation. Make time to listen today.

Discussion

1. How do we listen in prayer?

2. What tools help you to hear God's voice?

3. How do we guard against demonic influences in our prayer life?

Exercises

1. In your next time of prayer, meditate over a passage of scripture, one verse at a time. Read the verse aloud slowly, break it down into parts and repeat those. Record in your prayer journal insights which God gives you..

2. Sing some choruses and as you repeat the chorus focus on the meaning of the words. Let those words of praise sink into your heart.

3. Choose a good Christian book you always wanted to read. Read it with Jesus and discuss it together.

Notes

BREAKING THE ALABASTAR BOX

Lesson 17: Prayer Tips: Your Prayer Closet

Mt 6:6 But thou, when thou prayest, enter into thy closet, and when thou hast shut thy door, pray to thy Father which is in secret; and thy Father which seeth in secret shall reward thee openly.

Make no mistake, a prayer life is personal and private. Many Jews prayed at the temple, but Jesus did not recommend it. Not that corporate prayer is not important. Corporate prayer, like corporate worship, is for ministry to others. Our personal prayer life, however, is conducted in intimate privacy, just us alone with Jesus. For that, we need a prayer closet.

Jesus did not mean a literal "closet". Or at least not necessarily. Jesus was talking about a private place where you could conduct your personal relationship with him undisturbed by distractions. My prayer closet is my comfortable bedroom chair which I call affectionately, my "prayer chair". Your prayer closet needs to be your own personal place for quiet reflection and fellowship with the Lover of your soul. The place where you pray is uniquely yours and you should prepare it lovingly and with excitement.

First and foremost is privacy. We must have a place and time where we will not be disturbed. For me that is easy; I am at home alone most of the day. I can turn off the ringer on the phone and enjoy the peace of my sanctuary, my bedroom. For me, this is the perfect, comfortable, cozy place to spend time with Jesus.

That might not work for a lot of folks. If you work all day and spend the night with spouse and children all clamoring around you, it might seem as though there is no place you can hide. Yet there is no priority in your busy life which takes precedence over prayer. So, look around at your house and your calendar and get creative. Ask God to inspire you.

The objective is privacy. The first question is where. Where in your house is the most comfortable and private for you. It might even be the bathroom, where you can lock the door. You might have to set some rules about invading your prayer room. Maybe a sign which says, "Mamma at prayer".

Then we must establish the "when". Finding that quiet time to be alone with God might not be easy; in fact, it might be quite difficult. Yet, there is nothing we do with our time which yields richer results. So find some time - 30 minutes a day will do to start, although you should be forewarned, prayer is addictive and you will need more time soon. If you are a morning person, perhaps you could rise half an hour earlier. An evening person could stay up half an hour later. Perhaps there is half an hour of television you could pass up.. Or shorten some phone conversations. There is an old adage which says we make time for the things which are important to us. Prayer should be important.

Once you have decided upon your time and place, set those boundaries! Make sure everyone knows that you will not take calls or run errands, or otherwise be disturbed during prayer. Establishing the boundaries might take some time and effort, but your prayer life will be worth all the effort it takes.

After you have identified your time and space, it is time to feather the nest. Take the same interest in your prayer closet as you do any other part of your home. Make sure there is a comfortable place to sit. Provide adequate light. Your surroundings should be pleasant and peaceful; neat and orderly helps as well. Create a prayerful retreat to which you will eagerly retire each day.

Make your prayer closet a resourceful place. Fill your prayer area with spiritual resources which will aid in prayer. The helpful prayer aids listed in the previous lesson are a good idea. Don't forget your prayer journal and a pen. Some praise and worship music might put your in a praying mood. Make your prayer closet an easy and effective place to pray.

When we establish a place and time for prayer, prayer will happen. Planning and preparation take our commitment from desire to accomplishment. I challenge you to find your prayer closet today!

Discussion

1. What makes a good prayer closet?

2. How are private and public prayer different?

3. What is the best time to schedule your private prayer?

Exercises

1. Go through your home with an eagle eye and choose your prayer closet. Make it comfortable, attractive and private.

2. Take out a weekly calendar and write down a period of at least half an hour and commit to that time of prayer.

3. At your appointed time, go to your appointed place, and PRAY.

Notes

BREAKING THE ALABASTAR BOX
Lesson 18: Prayer Tips: Prayer and Fasting

Mt 17:21 Howbeit this kind goeth not out but by prayer and fasting.

No prayer life is complete without fasting. Yet, no aspect of prayer is so frustrating. The word "fasting" carries connotations of failure and condemnation. This is because no aspect of prayer is as little understood as that of fasting.

Perhaps it will help to understand what fasting is not. Fasting is not a way to twist God's arm. Fasting does not change God, it changes us. We do not fast in order to get God's attention or influence him to grant our petition. God loves us and only needs faith to loose power into our situation. Fasting helps us get our flesh under control. Fasting prepares us to hear from God. When we control the flesh, we free the spirit.

Fasting is not a way to elevate our holiness through suffering. Many Christians throughout the centuries have somehow gotten the notion that the more we suffer, the holier we are. Many of us feel that if we are miserable, we are closer to God. Nothing could be farther from the truth. Colossians 2:23 warns against neglecting our bodies in a demonstration of false holiness. Fasting is not meant to hurt our bodies, but to help us control them. We might not always enjoy self-discipline, but it will never harm us.

With that in mind, a diabetic should not stop taking medication in order to be able to fast. No one should be pressured or condemned into fasting for a week if they have never fasted a whole day.. Fasting is not a competition or an endurance trial.

Fasting is not something about which we brag. Jesus

instructed us to continue to be well groomed and avoid letting others know when we are fasting. This does not mean that we cannot participate in group fasting and share pertinent information. Yet our fasting, especially the successes, should be private. Becoming boastful about fasting defeats the purpose of fasting, which is to control the flesh.

Now that we know what fasting is not about, how do we add fasting to our prayer life? First of all, fasting does not have to be food. Any self-disciplinary activity which brings our carnal self under control will aid our prayer life. However, Jesus emphasized fasting, because eating is universal. We all eat, so we can all benefit from the self-discipline of fasting food. Disciplining our food helps us discipline other areas of our life as well.

Nor does fasting have to mean total abstinence from food of any kind. Biblical fasts included fasting from food that you like, or from meat, as in the three Hebrew children. If you are a beginner, or diabetic, or have other reasons why fasting is especially difficult, these fasts might be good choices for you.

Beginners should begin small. A one meal fast is still good self-discipline. When missing one meal becomes easy, it's time to go for two. Stay just beyond your comfort zone, just as you would in exercise or any other kind of discipline.

Fasting without prayer loses it's focus. Yes, we are reining in the flesh, but with nothing to put in its place. Perhaps this is one reason so many beginning fasters become frustrated. Disciplining the flesh prepares the way for the Spirit to be released during the time of prayer.

Usually, there will be no overwhelming insights from one session of prayer and fasting. Changing me takes time. In fact, that is the reason why fasting speeds our answers. The more easily I can control my flesh, the more easily I can find the mind of God.

Don't be afraid to add fasting to your prayer life. God does not expect perfection, only progress. Just think what benefit's a little self-discipline could bring!

Discussion

1. Would you call yourself a fasting crawler, walker, jogger, or sprinter?

2. Have you had a positive or negative experience with fasting in the past?

3. What benefits have you received from fasting?

4. What type of fast works best for you?

5. What would you like to gain from fasting?

Exercises

1. Using your prayer journal, make an inventory of undisciplined areas in your life.

2. Write a commitment to a fast, after careful consideration of which type and how long a
Fast you are ready to do. Commit this fast for one of the above areas in your life.

3. Pray over this commitment, then set a date.

4. Prepare for that date by arranging every thing you will need (special food, drink, etc).

5. On your appointed day, fast and pray and record your observations. Schedule another fast.

Notes

BREAKING THE ALABASTAR BOX

Conclusion

Col 4:2 Continue in prayer, and watch in the same with thanksgiving;

We have explored the fringes of the wonderful world of prayer. Now it is time to practice what we have explored. It is time to continue in prayer with thanksgiving.

I want my prayer life to be more than a mere habit. I want my prayer life to be ingrained inside me. Something I could not live without. Because I can't.

I want to continue in prayer; I want prayer to flow from me every day. Of course, a life of prayer starts with a habit. I have to discipline my flesh before I can free my spirit. I intend to push through the barriers of carnality to a natural spontaneous prayer life.

I mean to be faithful to prayer, trusting it to solve every problem. My life must be governed by prayer. I cannot give up because an answer does not come when I expect. I must continue in prayer.

Continuing prayer is successful prayer. Patience and persistence pays off. Many times people give up on prayer just when the breakthrough is about to happen. I don't want prayer to be something I do; I want prayer to be something I am.

I want my entire day to be one unending conversation with Jesus.. I want to have a spirit of prayer all day. I want to be able to pray at the drop of a pin. I want to be instant in season and out of season. I want to be at ease when I talk with my Father.

I know that the best way to reach my prayer goals is simply to pray. Not every day will be easy or fun. Some days will just be hard work. But then, that is true of any relationship. So I want to continue in prayer.

I want to be successful in my prayer life. Thanksgiving is a cause of success and a reflection of success. Two things happen when I thank God for what he has done. First, thanksgiving brings my attention to the answers I have received. So many times I spend so much time complaining that I fail to notice my blessings. Sometimes, God is moving much more in a situation than I have realized. I don't want to miss it when does.

Thanksgiving releases faith into my heart and thus into my prayers. As I thank him, I feel faith rising up inside me. Giving thanks is fun. Thanksgiving makes prayers exciting. I want always to pray with a thankful heart.

That has been the point of this Bible study. My goal has been to embed prayer into the lives of all who participate. May your time here be fruitful and yield a harvest of blessing. Keep on praying!

Discussion

1. What have you learned from this Bible study?

2. How has your prayer life changed?

3. Is there something you would still like to lean?

Exercises

1. Reread your prayer journal over the period of this Bible study. Note answered prayers. Note how you have grown spiritually..

2. Record your prayer goals for the coming months. How do you want your prayer life to grow?

3. Make a commitment to God to grow your prayer life.

Notes

www.ingramcontent.com/pod-product-compliance
Ingram Content Group UK Ltd.
Pitfield, Milton Keynes, MK11 3LW, UK
UKHW041926190726
13854UKWH00003B/1462